© Aladdin Books Ltd 2006

Designed and produced by
Aladdin Books Ltd
2/3 Fitzroy Mews
London W1T 6DF

Printed in Malaysia

First published in 2006 by
Franklin Watts
338 Euston Road
London NW1 3BH

Franklin Watts Australia
Hachette Children's Books
Level 17/207 Kent Street
Sydney NSW 2000

ISBN 0-7496-6822-9

ISBN 978-0-7496-6822-8

A catalogue record for this
book is available from the
British Library

Dewey Classification: 725'.18

The **author**, Margaret Mulvihill, was born in Ireland and lives in London.
She is the author of numerous articles for historical magazines and
books as well as two novels and a biography.
The **consultant**, Simon James, is a specialist on Roman history
and works for the Education Office at the British Museum.

Revised edition published in 2006
Original edition published as History Highlights – Roman Forts
Back cover: Hadrian's Wall, northern England
Design: David West Children's Book Design
Editor: Harriet Brown
Illustrator: Gerald Wood
Map: Aziz Khan
Picture researcher: Cecilia Weston-Baker

Contents

HALLMARKS OF HISTORY
Roman Forts

Aladdin/Watts
London • Sydney

Introduction

The time of the Roman Empire was one of prosperity and peace for Europe, North Africa and Asia Minor. The Roman Empire had a common law, and Latin and Greek were the official languages. People of many different cultures lived as Roman citizens. The peace was kept by the Roman army.

The Romans built forts which the soldiers used as bases. They patrolled frontiers and roads from them and even lived in them in the winter.

The first Roman emperor was called Augustus. He was a great nephew of Julius Caesar. Augustus reigned for nearly 50 years and brought peace after years of strife. He re-organised law and taxation and changed the armies into a professional peace-keeping force.

The Roman army marched through the centre of Rome. Augustus boasted that he had found Rome a city of brick and left it a city of marble.

The Roman Empire

At its largest, the Roman Empire included the whole of the Mediterranean world and stretched from Britain in the north and Arabia in the south-east. This huge territory included the Celts, Iberians, Greeks, Egyptians and others.

THE ROMAN EMPIRE

ASIA MINOR

Rome

Greece

MEDITERRANEAN SEA

NORTH AFRICA

Egypt

The Roman army

The Roman army was well-trained and equipped. Every soldier knew what his position was and where he should fight in battle. Augustus' army was made of 28 legions.

The most important officers in a legion were the centurions. There were about 60 centurions to a legion. Some were very brutal. There were also technical officers, such as engineers, medics and surveyors. An army of clerks organised how to pay, feed and equip the soldiers.

The Roman army relied on many native soldiers. Numidians from Africa and Gauls from France were better horsemen than Romans or Italians. The best archers came from Crete and the Balearic Islands.

Strict teachers taught the Roman recruits to march and run, leap, swim and ride, and to use their weapons in attack and defence. Every legion had a silver eagle – the symbol of the Roman Empire – as its standard. Individual units would have additional flags and badges, featuring zodiac signs or animals like wolves and boars. The loss of a standard was regarded as a disgrace.

A Roman legion

Each Roman legion was divided into units. Ten sections of eight men made up a century. Six centuries comprised a cohort (480 men) and ten cohorts made up a legion. Each cohort had its own battle order. Some 120 cavalrymen were attached to each legion. They were scouts and dispatch riders.

Cohorts

Cavalry

5 Tribuni

Legatus

Praefectus

Centurion

Aquilifer

Standard bearer

Senior officer

Centurion

Trumpeter

The Roman soldier

In the earliest days of Rome each citizen had to be prepared to fight without being paid. But soldiers in the Roman Empire were paid professionals who signed for 20-25 years of service. They often had to march 32 km a day.

Living conditions were simple and basic. In the field eight men would share a tent and a pack mule. In a fort, they shared two rooms. One was for sleeping and one was for storing equipment. Much of a soldier's time was spent on patrols or on sentry duty. Soldiers would be moved around the Empire as they were needed, from Britain to Africa.

Legionaries return to the fort from a patrol. During their time off duty, soldiers would play games or go to the baths. The soldiers, right, are playing with bones. Playing dice for money was not allowed but many ignored this rule.

Armour and weapons

Over his woollen tunic an ordinary legionary wore a metal breastplate. He had heavy studded sandals and a helmet. In cold conditions, he could stuff his sandals with wool and fur and he would be given a heavy cloak. A foot soldier had a short sword, two javelins and a heavy shield of leather and wood. Although there were repair workshops attached to each legion, much of the army's equipment came from Gaul and northern Italy.

Camps and forts

At the end of a day's march, Roman army units built a camp. Some officers were sent ahead to find clear, level ground, which could not be overlooked by enemies, near a supply of water.

Camps were usually square or rectangular. A deep trench was dug around the site. The turf was made into a bank over seven metres high. Soldiers set up their stakes on top of this rampart. Tents were pitched inside the camp. The headquarters included the commander and senior officers' tents and the standards. The soldiers' tents were pitched in rows around this area.

The legionary bases followed the same layout as the camps. The bases were permanent and often used as winter headquarters when the army was not on the move.

A permanent legionary base

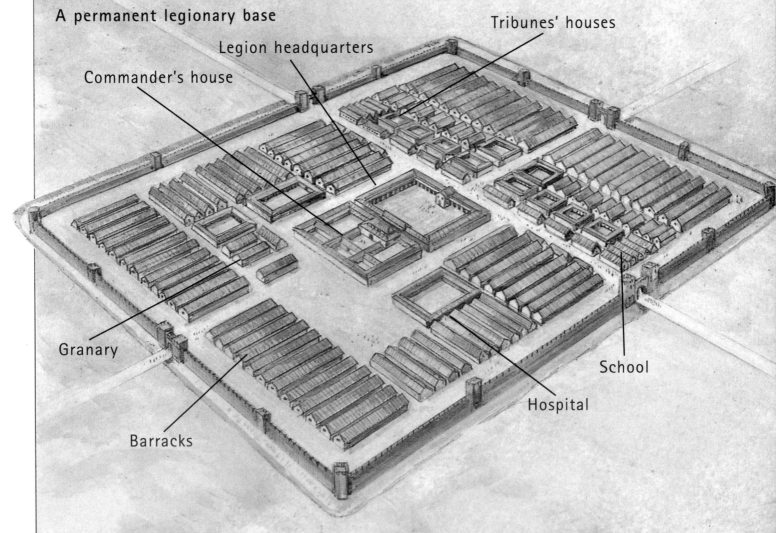

Commander's house

Legion headquarters

Tribunes' houses

Granary

Barracks

Hospital

School

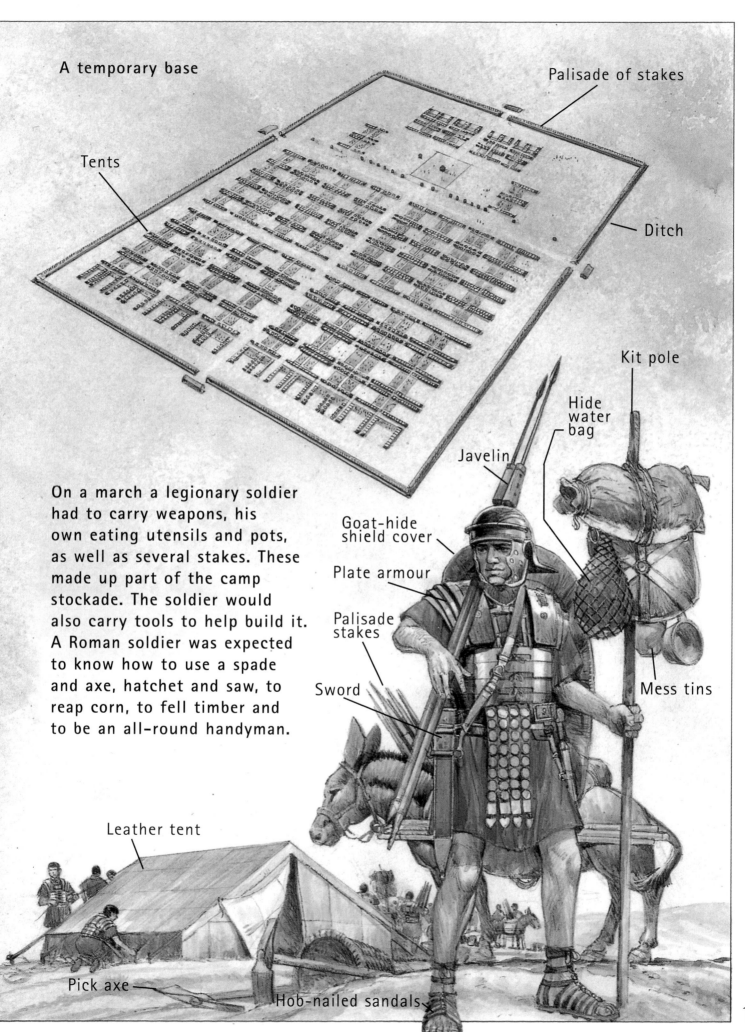

A temporary base

Palisade of stakes

Tents

Ditch

Kit pole

Hide water bag

Javelin

Goat-hide shield cover

Plate armour

Palisade stakes

Sword

Mess tins

On a march a legionary soldier had to carry weapons, his own eating utensils and pots, as well as several stakes. These made up part of the camp stockade. The soldier would also carry tools to help build it. A Roman soldier was expected to know how to use a spade and axe, hatchet and saw, to reap corn, to fell timber and to be an all-round handyman.

Leather tent

Pick axe

Hob-nailed sandals

Inside a Roman fort

As the Roman Empire stopped expanding, permanent forts were built for the legions in frontier zones. These forts had stone or wooden walls. The ramparts were made of timber and earth.

The fort's main road led to the central headquarters (principia) – the commander's house (praetorium), granaries and the hospital (valetudinarium). In the principia there was often a large hall, which contained the shrine for the standards. Forts also had workshops, stables and a small prison.

In a hot African fort more room was allowed for each soldier's bed and a large courtyard served as the hall. The British barrack block had to have a fireplace.

The Romans knew that diet, exercise and hygiene are important for general health. Senior officers had servants to house-keep for them. Ordinary soldiers had to keep themselves and their quarters clean and tidy. The centurions gave out chores, and made sure that the work was done.

The Bath-house

Bath-houses were attached to every fort. The water was heated by a furnace. Soldiers moved from a tepid room to a hot room, and from the sweat room to the cold bath. The soldiers would rub oil onto their skin to clean themselves. In the hot room they would sweat and scrape the dirt off. The baths were like a clubhouse, where soldiers would enjoy a few games and a bit of gossip.

Defending a Roman fort

Fort security was strict. Every day, there was a different watchword written on waxed pieces of wood. An officer called the tesserius organised the sentries and passed on this watchword. Each night, four legionary cavalrymen inspected the watchmen. If all was in order they took the watchwords ('tesserae') from the sentries on duty. At daybreak, the inspection party reported to the officer in charge, and handed over the wooden tablets. If a sentry was found guilty of falling asleep he was sentenced to being attacked with stones and sticks. Such men usually died. If they didn't they were disgraced forever.

To communicate with other forts or units along the frontier, the Romans used smoke signals. From special towers they burnt straw by day, and by night they used torch signals. The signalling tower had to be high enough for fire or smoke to rise clear of trees or mist.

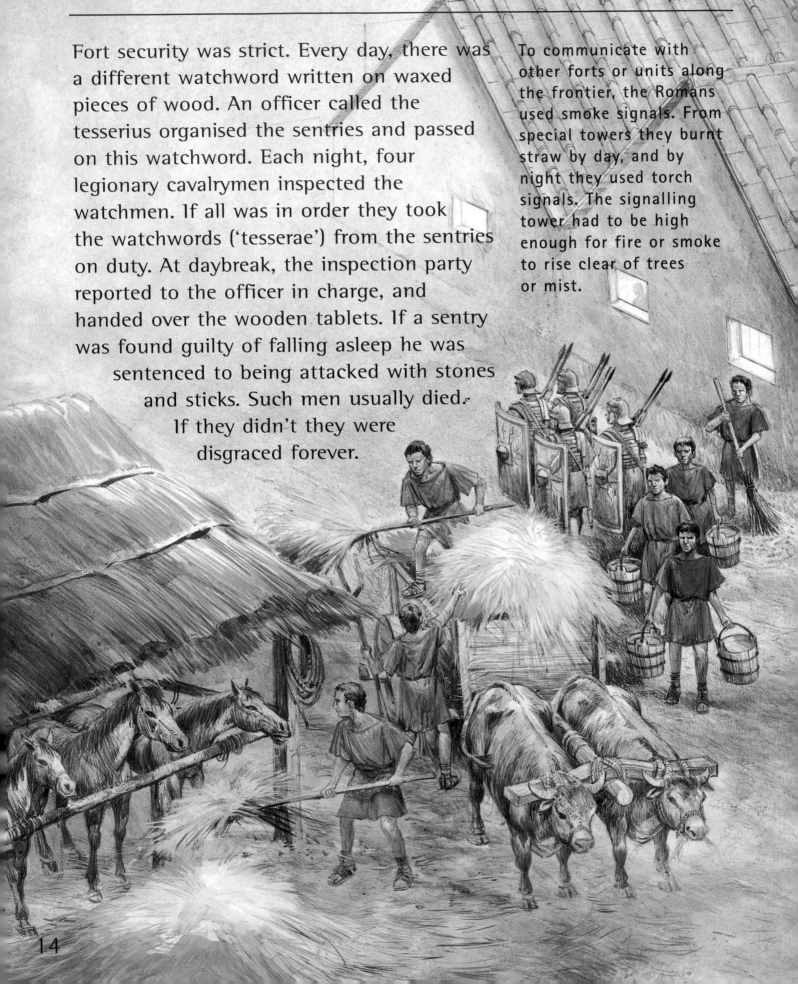

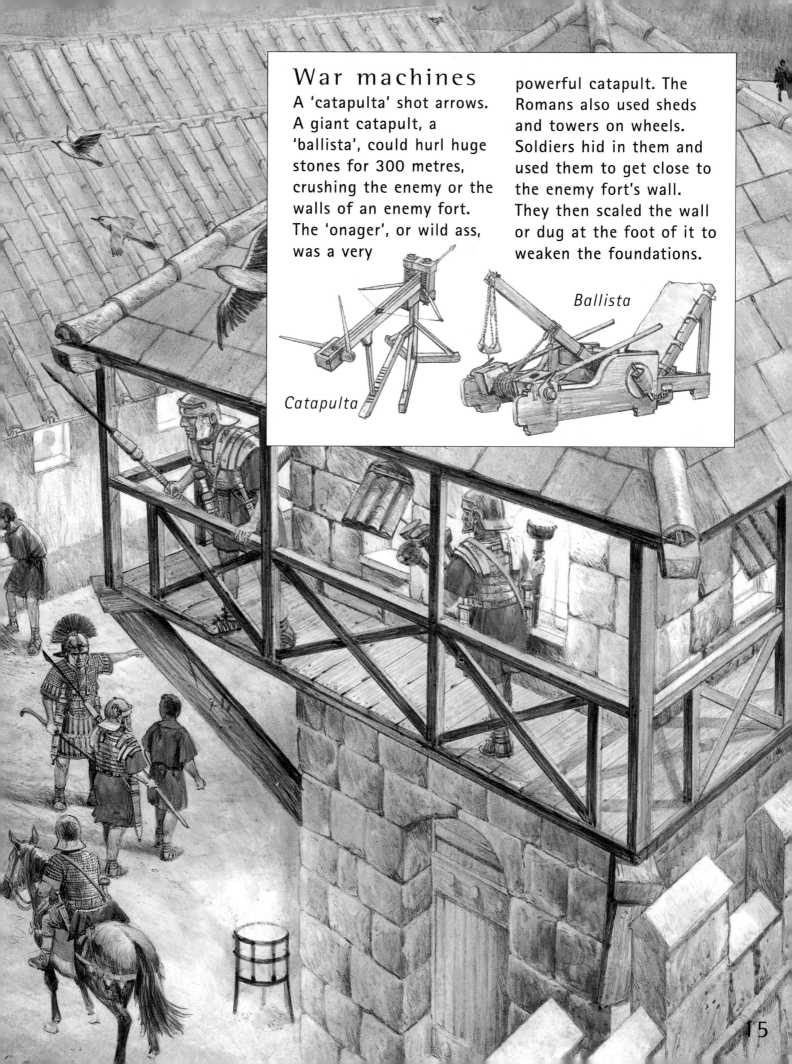

War machines

A 'catapulta' shot arrows. A giant catapult, a 'ballista', could hurl huge stones for 300 metres, crushing the enemy or the walls of an enemy fort. The 'onager', or wild ass, was a very powerful catapult. The Romans also used sheds and towers on wheels. Soldiers hid in them and used them to get close to the enemy fort's wall. They then scaled the wall or dug at the foot of it to weaken the foundations.

Catapulta

Ballista

15

Outside a Roman fort

The forts could be as large as 20-25 hectares, but they were strictly for soldiers and military business. Often, only the bath-house and an amphitheatre were built beyond the walls. The amphitheatre was used for gladiator fights, parades and ceremonies.

The area around a fort was called the canabae or booths. A large garrison attracted local traders. They set up their stalls outside a fort. At the stalls and taverns, soldiers enjoyed their leave. When they retired, soldiers didn't want to leave the areas they had settled in. They joined their families in their homes near the canabae.

Roman soldiers could buy trinkets outside the fort, or get letter-writers to send a message home. The booths' commander made sure that the businesses didn't get in the way of the fort's defences. Eventually, the people from the booths could apply for a charter and become a recognised settlement, or vicus. Many towns began like this.

Amphitheatre

The chance to see a real gladiator fight was a special occasion. The winning gladiator would ask the crowd if it wanted the loser's life to be spared. The crowd showed their palms up for 'yes' and thumbs down for 'no'.

Roads and engineers

The Romans built superb roads. They were always as straight as possible. The roads cut through hills and rocks with the aid of tunnels, and crossed rivers with bridges and viaducts. Some were cut into cliff sides. Sometimes they were paved with flat stone blocks or hard-packed gravel. On marshy grounds, foundations of logs were laid under the final surface.

These soldiers are building a road and there is an aqueduct in the background. Many of the roads are still in use. It was not until the 18th century that roads of this quality were seen again in Europe. Roman roads are the most universal and unmistakable evidence of Roman civilisation.

Bridges

This bridge at Cordoba in Spain is still in use. These military bridges were designed to last. The keystone in the middle of the arch had to be very strong. The Romans built many aqueducts – artificial channels for conveying water from rivers to houses and baths.

Good roads were essential for the movement of troops and supplies, for trade and for the postal service. Roman roads had frequent milestones and at 19 km intervals there were post-houses where travellers could stay overnight and where cavalrymen, the highway patrol, dispatch riders and official travellers could change their horses.

At the foot of the Forum in Rome, Augustus had a golden milestone set up. All roads ran toward the heart of the Empire.

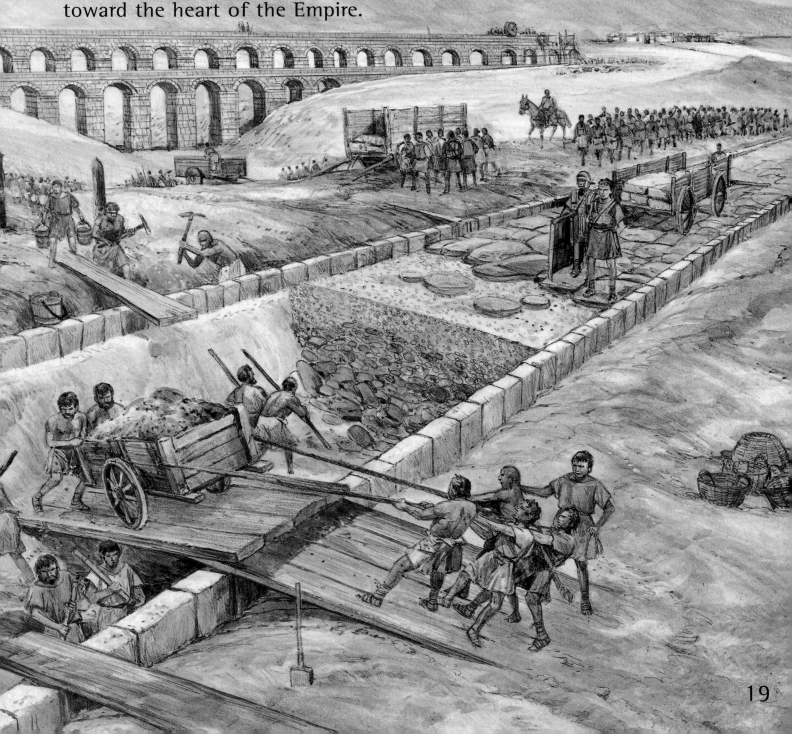

Religion

The Roman religion had Jupiter, Minerva, Vesta and Mars as some of its chief gods and goddesses. These gods were sacrificed to on particular occasions. Before military campaigns, for example, a public sacrifice might be made to Mars, the god of war. The first emperor, Augustus, was made into a god after he died. In remote parts of the Empire, some emperors were also worshipped as gods. Within the Empire a whole range of religions were allowed as long as they did not openly challenge the official cults and the emperor's divinity.

Christianity became the official religion of the Roman Empire in the 4th century, during the reign of the Emperor Constantine.

Many legionaries followed the cult of Mithras because it put great emphasis on comradeship between men. Followers of Mithras were expected to show brotherly love regardless of their status in the world.

Priests

This shows a priest making a sacrifice. The priests (haruspices) attached to each legion supervised the ceremonies in the military calendar. The emperor's birthday, or the anniversary of a legion's foundation, for example, would be celebrated by a sacrifice: a bull to Jupiter, a cow to Minerva, a young bull for the emperor.

Government

The Roman Empire was divided into provinces under Senate control and provinces that fell under the control of the emperor. The older provinces were ruled by proconsuls elected by the Senate. Newly conquered provinces, such as Britannia, were ruled through legates (deputies) appointed by the emperor. The emperor controlled the senators, a gathering of rich noblemen who filled most of the top posts in government and the army. Native Romans and Italians took most of the senior administrative jobs until well into the 2nd century.

The Emperor Hadrian inspecting one of his outlying forts. Hadrian is famous for having built Hadrian's Wall in England to protect it from northern invasions.

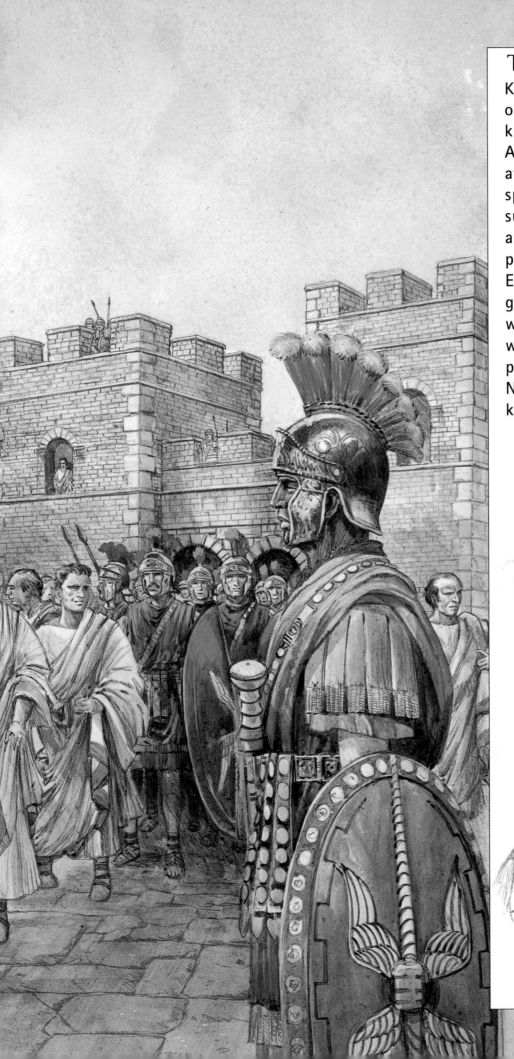

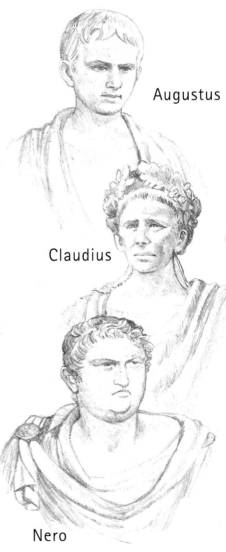

The emperors

Knowing that the citizens of Rome were suspicious of kings, the first emperor, Augustus, was careful to avoid personal wealth and splendour. But Augustus' successors were regarded as somewhere between the people and the gods. The Emperor Claudius was a grandson of Augustus' wife. Claudius' fourth wife was Agrippina, who poisoned him so her son, Nero, would succeed. Nero killed himself in AD 68.

Augustus

Claudius

Nero

Citizens and slaves

During the reign of Augustus, Roman citizenship was a privilege. A citizen of the Empire had many legal rights and privileges. Provincials or non-citizens fell under a second-class law called the 'ius gentium'. However, early in the 3rd century, all free men living within the Empire became citizens.

The Roman Empire depended on millions of slaves, who did the hardest and dirtiest work. Educated Greek slaves were often employed as teachers in noble families. Slaves did much of the administrative work. By imperial times slaves had some rights. More important, they could expect to become free men eventually.

Rome offered an orderly, prosperous life as a citizen. Invading barbarians offered chaos. If a treaty could not be made, or if they could not be encouraged to settle peacefully in a fixed place within the Empire, these war-like land-hungry tribes had to be overcome militarily.

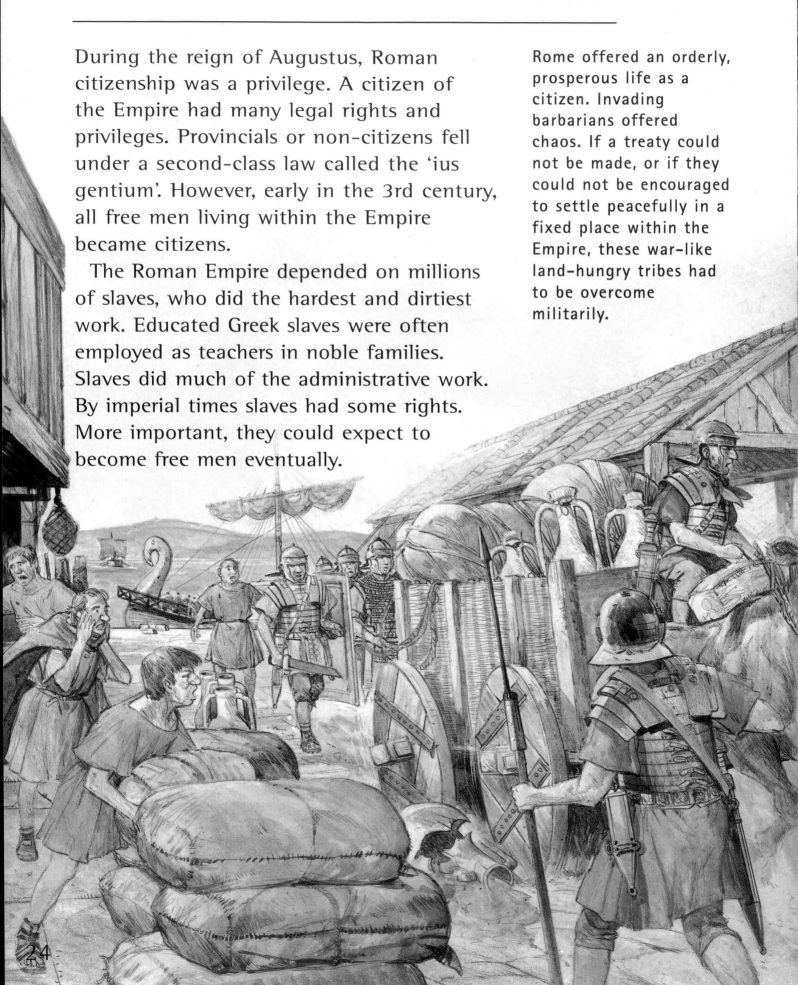

The toga

The toga was a half circle of white material wrapped around the body. The left end was carried over the left arm. The toga was the badge of Roman citizenship. It was so cumbersome and difficult to keep clean that it was only worn on public and formal occasions. A great event in the life of a Roman boy was the day he put on the 'toga virilis', the toga of manhood. He went to the Forum where his name was then added to the list of citizens.

What became of Roman forts?

Under Trajan (AD 98–117) the Empire grew too big to be easily defended. The next emperor, Hadrian, gave up some of Trajan's conquests and strengthened existing boundaries.

The third century saw frequent problems. The forts could not keep out invasions forever. Germanic tribes came over the Rhine, while Persians came from the east.

In AD 285 the Empire was divided in two and the emperors had to be full-time military leaders. The army became weakened by constant wars. In 476 the last western emperor was removed by German commanders. Only the eastern half of the Empire endured until its capture by Turks, in 1453.

The Romans occasionally used existing hillforts as the basis for their own forts. When the Roman soldiers abandoned their forts, the local people would then take over the sites and build their own towns around them.

Hadrian's Wall

Hadrian's Wall runs for 112 km from Wallsend-on-Tyne to Bowness-on-Solway. It was built in the AD 120s after a visit by the Emperor. He wanted to protect this northerly defence from attack by Picts. The wall was 2.7 m thick and 5.8 m high. It had 80 small castles and a fort every 6–10 km. It had to be rebuilt several times before being abandoned in the 4th century.

The Roman Empire today

The Roman legacy lived on in Christianity, and many languages – Italian, French, Spanish, Romanian – grew from a common Latin source. Latin words make up more than half of the words we use in English – we speak of the salary a person receives 'per annum', for example. 'Arena' means sand since the amphitheatres were usually covered with sand. Other ordinary everyday examples are 'omen', 'specimen', 'actor' and 'circus'. In Britain, place names ending in 'chester' come from 'castrum' (camp).

For centuries and centuries after the death of the last western emperor, Rome continued to be a civilising influence. Ruins like Dougga in Tunisia remained as a physical reminder of its grandeur. The cultural and political legacy has been permanent.

Roman influence

When people think of civilisation, classical Roman buildings come to mind. Architects still draw inspiration from Roman buildings. Churches were built with Roman arches throughout Europe until a new style of pointed arches began in the 11th century. This library building in Oxford, England, owes a lot to Roman design. The founders of modern America were also influenced by Roman civilisation. They used words like 'senate', 'constitution' and 'republic'.

Date Charts

31 BC Victory for Octavian at the Battle of Actium.

27 BC Octavian became Augustus and the Roman Empire began.

14 AD Death of Augustus.

c. 33 AD Crucifixion of Jesus Christ.

41 AD Emperor Caligula murdered by Praetorians.

43 AD Roman conquest of southern Britain.

66 AD Jews in Palestine revolted against Roman rule.

68 AD Death of Nero.

79 AD Destruction of Pompeii by eruption of Vesuvius.

80 AD Completion of the Colosseum in Rome.

117 AD Death of Trajan; accession of Hadrian.

122 AD Beginning of Hadrian's Wall.

161–66 AD War against the Parthians. Plague followed.

212 AD Roman citizenship granted to all free males of the Empire.

230s AD onwards Wars with Persia. Barbarian invasions.

253–68 AD Germanic barbarians invaded.

284 AD Accession of Diocletian, who re-organised the Empire.

312 AD Constantine became emperor.

313 AD Edict of Milan, Christianity tolerated within Empire.

367 AD Successful attack on Roman Britain by Picts, Scots and Saxons.

378 AD Goths defeated and killed eastern Roman emperor Valens.

410 AD Rome captured by Alaric the Goth; around this time Roman rule ended in Britain.

415 AD Visigoths began conquest of Spain.

476 AD Romulus Augustulus, last western Roman emperor deposed by Odovacar, a barbarian leader.

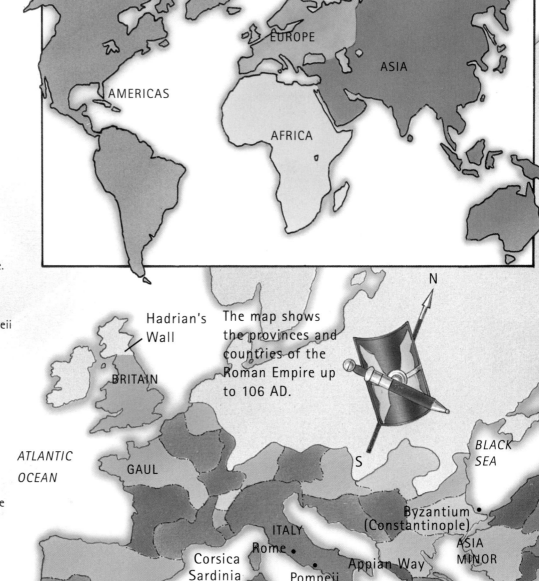

The map shows the provinces and countries of the Roman Empire up to 106 AD.

Africa	Asia	Americas	Europe
	63 BC Judea made a Roman province.	**100 BC** Beginning of the rise of Teotihuacan, great city in Mexico.	**27 BC** Octavian becomes emperor; the Roman Empire begins.
10 AD Kushite Kingdom in Nubia in decline.	**25 AD** Beginning of Han Dynasty in China.		**14 AD** Augustus dies.
	c33 AD Crucifixion of Jesus Christ.		
	c58-75 AD Buddhism accepted as official religion in China.		**64 AD** Fire in Rome.
	66 AD Jews in Palestine revolt against Roman rule.		**79 AD** Eruption of Vesuvius destroys Pompeii.
	c100 AD Paper invented in China.		**117 AD** Death of Trajan; accession of Hadrian.
	220 AD End of Han Dynasty in China.		**161-66 AD** The Romans fight the Parthians.
	230 AD Emperor Sujin rules Japan; first written records there.		**212 AD** Roman citizenship given to all free men.
c300 AD Axum (ancestor of Ethiopia) becomes the dominant power in the Red Sea.	**309-79 AD** Persian power at its height under Shapur II.	**300 AD** Classic Mayan civilisation established in Mesoamerica.	**230s AD** Wars with Persia; barbarian invasions.
			253-68 AD Germanic barbarians invade the Empire.
300s AD Axum converts to Christianity.	**320 AD** Gupta Dynasty reunites India.		**284 AD** Diocletian begins to reorganise the Empire.
	c350 AD Pallava Dynasty set up in south India.		**313 AD** Christianity tolerated within the Empire.
	c360 AD Japan conquers Korea.		
		c400 AD Incas start to establish themselves on the South American coast.	
429 AD Vandal Kingdom of North Africa is set up.			**410 AD** Rome captured by Alaric the Goth.
			476 AD Romulus Augustulus, last Western Roman emperor deposed by Odovacar.
	560 AD Birth of Muhammad.		

Glossary

canabae 'booths', the settlement around a fort.

castrum 'camp'.

century a unit of the Roman army consisting of 80 men.

cohort six centuries or 480 men. A legion had ten cohorts.

haruspices the priests attached to legions.

ius gentium the legal system of non-citizens.

papilio 'butterfly', the nickname for an army tent.

praetorium the commander's house in a fort.

principia headquarters in a camp or fort.

sacellum the shrine in which legionary standards were kept.

tessera waxed wooden tablet on which the daily password was written; the tesserius was the officer in charge of the passwords.

toga virilis 'toga of manhood' worn by Roman boys at their coming of age.

vicus a permanent settlement of retired soldiers.

Index

Photographic credits:
Pages 9, 12, 16, 18, 25 and 28: Michael Holford Photography; page 20: Werner Forman Archive; pages 27 and the back cover: J. Allan Cash Library.